YOU CHO

EARLY AMERICAN BATTLES

AT THE BATTLE OF YORKTOWN

AN INTERACTIVE BATTLEFIELD ADVENTURE

by Eric Braun

Consultant:
Richard Bell, PhD
Associate Professor of History
University of Maryland, College Park

CAPSTONE PRESS
a capstone imprint

You Choose Books are published by Capstone Press,
1710 Roe Crest Drive, North Mankato, Minnesota 56003
www.mycapstone.com

Library of Congress Cataloging-in-Publication Data
Library of Congress Cataloging-in-Publication data is available on the Library of
Congress website.

978-1-5435-0289-3 (library binding)
978-1-5435-0293-0 (paperback)
978-1-5435-0297-8 (eBook PDF)

Editorial Credits
Adrian Vigliano, editor; Bobbie Nuytten, designer;
Kelli Lageson, media researcher; Kathy McColley, production specialist

Photo Credits
Alamy: David Stuckel, 16, Louis S. Glanzman, 73; Bridgeman Images: Peter
Newark American Pictures/Private Collection/Pyle, Howard (1853-1911), Cover,
Private Collection/Troiani, Don (b.1949), 10, 20, 34, 40, 98; Getty Images: Archive
Photos, 62, Interim Archives, 102; Library of Congress Prints and Photographs
Division: 57; Newscom: Ann Ronan Picture Library Heritage Images, 13, World
History Archive, 6; North Wind Picture Archives: 25, 68, 79, 83, 93; Shutterstock:
Alexey Pushkin, Design Element, Atlantis Images, Design Element, Everett
Historical, 48, Lukasz Szwaj, Design Element; Wikimedia: http://www.aoc.gov/cc/
photo-gallery/ptgs_rotunda.cfm, 66

Printed in the United States of America.
010830S18

Table of Contents

About Your Adventure 5

Chapter 1

Weary of War 7

Chapter 2

French Fighter 11

Chapter 3

Fighting for Freedom 41

Chapter 4

War Heroine 69

Chapter 5

From Siege to Surrender 99

Timeline 106

Other Paths to Explore 108

Read More 109

Internet Sites 109

Glossary 110

Bibliography 111

Index 112

ABOUT YOUR ADVENTURE

You are living in the year 1781. The American war for independence from British rule rages all around you. People around the world wait to see which side will emerge victorious.

In this book you'll explore how the choices people made meant the difference between life and death. The events you'll experience happened to real people.

Chapter One sets the scene. Then you choose which path to read. Follow the directions at the bottom of each page. The choices you make will change your outcome. After you finish your path, go back and read the others for new perspectives and more adventures.

YOU CHOOSE the path
you take through history.

WEARY OF WAR

You sit in front of your tent in a large, bustling camp in New York. Activity is all around you. Massive pots boil over open fires and men — sweating in the summer heat — rush between the tents. You hear excited talk, hollers, and even the occasional laugh. Horses whinny while hundreds of soldiers sleep, eat, and, like you, await their orders. General George Washington is in camp too, though you have yet to see the great leader.

Turn the page.

America's war for independence from Great Britain has been going on for six years and everyone is exhausted. You have seen friends killed in battle as well as frozen and starved to death in the brutal winters. You find yourself wondering if independence is really worth it.

But today there is a new feeling in the humid air — a feeling of excitement. Washington has planned a sneak attack on British forces stationed in Yorktown, Virginia. The French navy has attacked and weakened the British navy on the Chesapeake Bay, where Yorktown is located. Striking now and taking back the town could bring an end to the war.

Your commander approaches. It is time to move out. Your stomach boils with the usual anxiety about battle — and a thrill that victory may be at hand.

To be a French officer fighting with the patriots, turn to page 11.

To be an African-American slave who has been promised freedom in exchange for fighting, turn to page 41.

To be a woman working in the Continental Army, turn to page 69.

CHAPTER 2

FRENCH FIGHTER

You have been a soldier in the French army for many years. You've fought bravely and sometimes been injured in European wars. After all these years, you have risen to the rank of captain. As you reach the end of your long career, you are well respected and loved by your men. They and your superiors consider you to be an intelligent, honorable soldier.

Because you have served France well, you were given the option to stay home from this war. You could have taken an easier assignment. But you could not resist coming to America to help defend the colonists from Britain.

Turn the page.

After all, the British are France's enemy. And you feel that the patriot cause is exciting and just. But you have been away from home for nearly three years. You keep thinking of your twin sons, Bastien and Paul. They are now 8 years old, though they were 5 years old the last time you saw them. You have seen many French soldiers, including men under your command, die for America. You want to win this war, but for the sake of your family, you do not want to end up joining the long list of the war dead.

For the past few days, General Rochambeau and General Washington have been talking about attacking New York City. But with the news that the French navy has defeated British ships near Yorktown, the plan has changed. Rochambeau holds an officers' meeting in his tent. French troops, along with the patriots, will be marching south to Yorktown starting tonight.

General George Washington and French General Rochambeau give orders to their men in 1781.

A small number of troops will also stay back to create a diversion. They will keep camp and make it look like all the troops are here.

Due to your seniority, you are given a choice. You may lead your army to Yorktown and help storm the town. Or you can stay here in New York and create the diversion.

To go to Yorktown, turn to page 14.

To stay in New York, turn to page 17.

Sharp spikes were placed around British outposts to help prevent enemy attacks.

"Please," the prisoner says. "You must stop your attack. In the town there is much suffering. Smallpox. No food. Even Americans suffer and die. Stop the shelling."

To have the man shackled to deal with him later, turn to page 19.

To bring the prisoner to General Rochambeau to discuss his plea, turn to page 27.

Your wife would be happy to know that you are taking the safer route. By staying in New York, you hope to avoid flying musket balls and live to see your sons again. But as you watch the other troops head off in the middle of the night, you feel a pang of guilt.

Through the night your men build bread ovens and keep them stoked. You burn fires, move around heavy equipment, and dig trenches. Your men make plenty of noise. The ruse is successful. According to a report from patriot spies, the British in New York are preparing for defense. They have no idea most of the allied armies have gone south.

It's good news indeed. The bad news is that you are very bored.

Turn the page.

That's when a messenger enters the camp on horseback. He calls to you and you wait as he dismounts. "Important news, sir!" he says.

The news is that a severe fever and rash has spread through one of the Continental army units. The men can't go on. They are returning to the New York camp now and will take over the diversion as best they can. You will have to join the fighting after all.

To prepare your men to leave immediately, turn to page 21.

To hold the post until the sick Americans return, turn to page 29.

The general does not need to be distracted right now. Of course the enemy is suffering—this is war. You have the redcoat shackled to a post and forget about him.

Finally, the shelling stops and General Washington gives the order: affix bayonets to muskets. After dark, you will sneak across the battle-scarred field. Sappers with axes will lead the way and cut through the abatis. The soldiers following them will attack without firing. The point is to be quick and quiet.

You are going to capture two critical outposts. The patriot Colonel Alexander Hamilton will take one of them. He gives a simple order to his men: "Follow me!" And they are off.

You turn to your own men and give a similar command: "Let's go!"

Turn the page.

A French soldier armed and prepared to fight.

You cross the field silently, and the sappers begin to hack away at the abatis. Suddenly a gunshot cracks, and your men hit the ground. A British sentry on the wall has seen you and fired. Luckily, no one was hit, but he is reloading now. And surely more redcoats will be joining him on that wall in a moment.

To keep to the plan, turn to page 23.

To order your men to fire back, turn to page 32.

There is no time to wait. If the attack is undermanned, it might fail. So you give the order and your unit immediately begins preparing to move out. Packs are filled, and ammunition is counted and parceled out. Horses are loaded down. In less than two hours, you are hiking in the woods, heading south.

You march for several days, foraging for food along the way. At Williamsburg, Virginia, you catch up to the other armies. After one night of rest, you are all on the move again. After making camp outside Yorktown, General Washington invites you and the other officers into his tent to discuss the plan.

There are two outposts dug into the earth outside the town, and you need to take them. The outposts are protected by palisades adorned with spiked stakes.

Turn the page.

Surrounding the palisades are moats and abatis — a field of treetops with branches sharpened to razor-sharp points. A unit of sappers, men with axes and pikes, will sneak out first and begin hacking apart the abatis. Infantry units will follow. Yours will be one of them.

Washington gives strict orders to attack quietly and only with bayonets — no shots fired. That would alert the British of your attack and ruin the surprise. But as your unit moves into the hacked-up abatis, someone shoots. You realize it's a guard up on the wall of the outpost. Some of the men get nervous, and one of them asks permission to fire back.

"Hold your fire," you say sharply. "Continue as planned."

Turn to page 23.

Your men remain silent as they creep up to the abatis. For the time being, the guard does not shoot again — perhaps he lost sight of you in the dark. The sappers keep hacking at the tangle of spikes and thorns.

Suddenly another shot comes down and one of your men is hit in the shoulder. He falls to the ground, and the other men duck as well. You scan their faces and see that they are scared. They feel exposed out here. They are itching to return fire or — even worse — run away.

All of the allied armies have had trouble with soldiers abandoning their posts. The war has been long and brutal. In a way, you cannot blame them. By simply walking into the woods, they can leave behind the dangers of war. They can return to their families. Who would not want to do that? You miss your family as well.

Turn the page.

But loyalty is critical for a soldier. If a few men leave, others may follow. Without a strong force, you risk losing the outpost. Then you risk losing Yorktown and perhaps the whole war.

The sappers are almost through the abatis now. It's almost time to rush the outpost. How will you ensure your troops are ready?

To inspire them with a speech, turn to page 25.

To lead by example and rush into battle, turn to page 34.

You stand tall. "Men," you say, "we have been in this war for a long time and I know you are tired. I know you have seen terrible things. I know you are hungry, and I know you have sacrificed. I also know you will be brave, because you *are* brave. We must be fierce now. Success here could mean an end to all of it."

Turn the page.

Tired, worn soldiers rest and warm up by a fire.

And then you give the agreed-on attack signal, which is the general's name: *Rochambeau.* You say it slowly so it comes out sounding like three words: "Row-sham-bow!"

Some of the soldiers stand up and nod in agreement. The others follow their example. "Let's go!" you yell, and you all pour through the opening in the abatis. The first men through begin to cross the moat and several of the men stumble and fall. Are they being shot? You did not hear gunfire, but you could have missed it in the excitement.

To rush across the moat and climb the wall first, turn to page 36.

To stay on the safe side of the moat and direct your men, turn to page 38.

The man is clearly in great pain and you believe that inside the town, others are suffering deeply. You bring him to the general.

At first, Rochambeau's assistant will not let you approach. "Get him out of here," he says, pointing to the prisoner. "The ground attack is about to begin and the general cannot be bothered at this important moment."

"But that is exactly why I must talk to him now, before the attack," you say. "There are Americans in the town too. Civilians are dying."

The assistant says, "Wait here." He goes to Rochambeau, who approaches you and the prisoner. You tell him what the redcoat told you and then the redcoat tells his story again.

Rochambeau strokes his beard. Finally he speaks. "Return to the town," he tells the man.

Turn the page.

"We will cease fire for one hour. Tell General Cornwallis we demand an immediate surrender." Rochambeau says that if the British do not surrender within the hour, he will release another volley of artillery.

The prisoner goes away into the night.

"I hope this is not a mistake," the general says to you coldly. And then he leaves.

An hour passes and there is no sign of the white surrender flag or of General Cornwallis. There is, however, news from the bay — the British ships containing reinforcements are nearly here. That hour may have cost you the chance for an easy victory. You have a sinking feeling in your gut that you have indeed made a terrible mistake.

THE END

To follow another path, turn to page 9.
To read the conclusion, turn to page 99.

It's not safe to leave the camp unprotected, so you wait. The next day the soldiers return. They look awful. Many are covered with a rash from head to foot. It is smallpox, and you realize that most of them will die. They won't do much good protecting this camp. You don't expect a British attack, but you decide to wait for a report from your spies to make sure.

In the meanwhile, the sick soldiers go to bed and wait to get better — or die. You hear them moaning in pain through the night. Your own soldiers begin to worry that they will be infected too. You realize this is a real danger. You keep your men on a far end of the camp, but some simply abandon their posts and go home. By the time you hear from your spies that the British will not attack, half a dozen of your men are sick.

Turn the page.

You begin the march toward Yorktown, but as the days go on, more men get sick. The march goes slower and slower. Soon you reach Williamsburg, where many allies are stationed. You meet with a patriot colonel at a public building. He tells you that the battle is already over. The French and Continental armies have taken Yorktown.

You are glad for the news, but your happiness is mixed with a warm feeling of disappointment building behind your eyes. You wish you had been there to help with the victory. Also, you are very thirsty. You drink a cup of water, but it doesn't seem to help.

Wait — a warmth behind your eyes? Sitting at the table with the colonel, you realize what that feeling really is. It's fever. Your armpit is very itchy, and you scratch it. Then you notice a bubbly rash on your arm.

You're sure it is smallpox.

You avoided combat in order to stay safe. But now you are likely to die anyway. "Sir," you say to the colonel. "Could you get me paper and a quill? I must write a letter to my family. I may never see them again."

THE END

To follow another path, turn to page 9.
To read the conclusion, turn to page 99.

You can't just sit there and let them fire on you, no matter what General Washington ordered. "Return fire!" you command.

The men shoot and a firefight breaks out. At the other outpost, Colonel Hamilton and his men take fire too. The allies are exposed by the abatis and many are shot. One falls near you and you rush to help him. He is bleeding from his chest and you realize there is nothing you can do.

You are filled with anger at yourself for losing your cool. You should have stuck with the sneak attack. But now there is no choice — you must get to the wall as soon as possible.

"Charge!" you yell, and the men rush through the hacked-up abatis. The outpost wall is cracked and torn apart from the artillery fire and you lead the men to one of the holes. A sapper chops it open wider with his axe and you rush inside.

Outside there was a bright moon, but inside it is darker. Suddenly a lantern comes toward you and someone yells a battle cry. Your men charge forward with bayonets into a fierce hand-to-hand fight. You suffer a gunshot to your hand, but soon the enemy is subdued. Many try to retreat through the rear of the outpost, but Washington has stationed men there. Those who try to escape are captured.

The outpost is now in allied hands, but the cost of life was much higher than it should have been. You are to blame. You know that Washington will be furious. Rochambeau may demote you. You can only wait to see what your fate will be.

THE END

To follow another path, turn to page 9.
To read the conclusion, turn to page 99.

With a yell, you climb the wall. A redcoat greets you atop the wall with a sword and you stab at him with your bayonet. He slashes your gut. You're bleeding badly, but you lunge at him again and he falls off the wall.

Your men rip through an opening in the wall, weakened from the artillery shelling, and quickly overwhelm the redcoats inside. You take one outpost while Colonel Hamilton takes the other. Prisoners are marched back to General Washington.

The sappers immediately begin to dig a trench that extends to the captured outposts. The artillery is wheeled in and you begin to shell the town.

The next day Cornwallis, the British general, surrenders. He and Washington work out the details and soon hundreds of British troops are marched out of the town. It is a proud moment. Still, you wonder if Great Britain will ever surrender entirely.

Months later, you step off a ship in the French port of La Rochelle. Your wife, Marie, and your children, Bastien and Paul, greet you with big smiles and hugs. Later, you are recognized by the government as a war hero and given a medal. You retire knowing that you helped defeat the British and establish a new, independent United States.

THE END

To follow another path, turn to page 9.
To read the conclusion, turn to page 99.

You need to stay safe so you can see your family again. You instruct the soldiers to attack while you stay back. They rush in. Soon you realize that they were not being shot. They were tripping in craters created by the artillery shelling, which they can't see in the dark.

Your men cross the moat and hack open a damaged part of the wall. The redcoats rain down gunfire. From your post on the far side of the moat, you see several of your soldiers fall.

Before long, the shooting stops. The outpost is taken. A cheer goes up from the allies.

Quickly, the sappers begin to dig a trench connecting to the outposts. When they're complete, they wheel in the artillery. They must act quickly to take the town before British reinforcements arrive.

Everyone is working hard together. But you sense that you have lost the loyalty of the men in your unit. It is clear you acted to keep yourself safe while letting them face all the danger.

Washington orders the artillery to fire on Yorktown. The town is taken quickly. This becomes the war's turning point. Soon it is all over and the United States is independent. Many of the leaders from the battle are recognized for their valor and heroism, but you are not. As a lifelong military man, it hurts to be passed over.

You return to be with your family and live in comfort. You mostly forget about your decision to let others rush in while you stayed back. It is only occasionally, late at night, that you think of the men who died in your place.

THE END

To follow another path, turn to page 9.
To read the conclusion, turn to page 99.

A soldier of the 1st Rhode Island Regiment in 1781. The 1st Rhode Island Regiment became known as the "Black Regiment" when it began allowing the recruitment of African Americans in 1778.

CHAPTER 3

FIGHTING FOR FREEDOM

The patriots want freedom for America. But what do they really know about freedom? You were born into slavery — owned by a rich white man in Rhode Island. When the patriots needed more soldiers, some slaves were sold into the Continental Army. You have been promised that when this war is over, you will be a free man.

There are a few problems with that promise. One, will they keep their word? In your experience, white men have not been very trustworthy. Two, what of your mother? She remains at Master Stevens' estate. Will she be freed?

Turn the page.

You wonder also about what will happen if you are killed. You have witnessed plenty of suffering in this war. You have seen many die, including your older brother, Jeremiah. When Jeremiah was shot and lay bleeding to death, you made him a promise. When the war is over, you will get your mother to freedom. Somehow. He gave you an old cloth band, which your mother used to tie back her hair. It still smells of her and you keep it in your pocket at all times.

For now you fight and you fight hard. It is your only choice. End this war and you have a chance at living a free life.

You are part of a unit of 140 slaves. You march for weeks, heading south from New York to Williamsburg, Virginia. This is where the armies all meet for the final push to Yorktown. Here, your unit is divided into two groups.

Sappers will have axes and shovels. They will clear away the enemy's protective wooden structures and dig trenches large enough to move artillery through. Infantrymen will go into combat with muskets and bayonets.

To be a sapper, turn to page 44.

To be in the infantry, turn to page 46.

Map of the Battle of Rhode Island, 1778. An accurate map could mean the difference between victory and defeat during the Revolutionary War.

You take his musket and shove him along. But later you ask an officer in your unit what is happening in Rhode Island. He says that a British army has been raiding plantations. While most of the men are away at war, the families are unprotected. The raiders are stealing food and other goods — and killing civilians.

You think of your mother. Is she safe?

To stay on duty, turn to page 52.

To abandon the army and return to your mother, turn to page 54.

48

You can't just stand here and let them shoot at you. At least if you join the attack, you have a chance. So you rush on with the infantry and enter the outpost through a crack in the wall. All you have is your ax, which isn't much of a weapon against a musket or a bayonet. But you are brave and you are fast. You rush into the fight.

Suddenly you recognize a man among the British troops. You knew him as a slave on a plantation next to yours. You would see him sometimes in the fields. It looks as though he ran away from slavery before you did — back when only the British were taking blacks in their army. He charges toward you with his musket raised. You don't want to fight him, but you're not sure if you have a choice.

To attack him, turn to page 56.

To say something, turn to page 59.

You figure you were lucky enough to be given a non-combat job in this battle. You might as well avoid the combat. Your mother already lost one of her sons. You don't want her to lose both of them.

You duck back into the abatis and stay as low as you can. Other sappers are doing the same. No more shots are coming your way, as the fighting is all taking place inside the shelters now. You're glad you made the safe choice.

It's not long before the attack is over and the officers have called you back to duty. You dig a trench to connect the rear trench with the newly captured outposts. You and the other sappers work hard and fast. Time is critical. The allies must take Yorktown before British reinforcements arrive. As you dig, you imagine you are prying up pile after pile of your own freedom.

When the trench is complete, you help wheel in one of the huge artillery cannons. General Washington is present to order the shelling of Yorktown from your new, safe position. The town falls quickly and the British general, Cornwallis, surrenders.

You are part of a crew that goes into the town to help collect loot from the surrender. Your team searches the courthouse, which the redcoats had used as a headquarters. In an upstairs room you find a purse with gold coins. And in several storage lockers, you find something even more valuable — food! You are so hungry that the idea of fresh food makes your knees tremble.

You look around. Nobody else is in the room.

51

To steal money and eat food, turn to page 60.

To report everything to the officers, turn to page 62.

It would take weeks to reach the plantation, especially since you don't have any money. Whatever danger your mother has faced, it is surely over by now. There isn't much you can do, so you stay on with the army. You want to earn your freedom.

Later, when the artillery is shelling Yorktown, an army of redcoats attacks the left flank. You fire on the enemy and hit one. Hiding in the trench, you quickly load a new musket ball and fire again. Another hit. "Good shooting!" the colonel says.

A few of your fellow soldiers are hit in the attack as the redcoats charge the trench. They spike some of the artillery, making them useless. Through the smoke and haze, you feel a shot hit you in the arm. But you manage to keep reloading and firing.

You charge into the teeth of the attack, fending off several redcoats. Soon the enemy is retreating back to Yorktown and the artillery barrage is back on.

Now that the battle has died down, you assess your injury. It's probably not life-threatening, but it hurts badly. You're lying far away from the trench, alone in the woods. You realize nobody knows where you are. You are probably presumed dead. You think again about taking your freedom now by running away.

Lying near you is a dead British soldier. Checking his satchel, you find a pocket watch, a few coins, dried meat, and a letter from his wife.

53

To take the satchel and run, turn to page 64.

To go back to camp, turn to page 66.

You can't trust the patriots to let you go when the war is over. Besides, if your mother is in danger, you have to get to her as soon as possible.

It's dawn as you finish processing the prisoners. The sappers are furiously digging a new trench for the artillery. You doze against the outpost wall for a while and listen to the picks and shovels slip into the soft earth. Occasionally they hit a rock and the loud sound startles you.

When you wake up, the sappers are rolling the cannons through the new trench. Soon, the shelling of the town begins. You stand guard against a ground attack but it does not come. Before long, the exploding artillery and crumbling town are just background noise to your thoughts of home. You wait until the officers are distracted with the ammunition supply and quickly disappear into the woods.

You walk for weeks. You travel only at night and avoid roads. Finally, exhausted and starving, you reach the old plantation. The main building is wrecked. One wing is burned to the ground and the entry hall is sagging and charred.

Worst of all, there is no sign of your mother or anyone else. You slump against the wall of your old home and begin to cry.

When you regain your composure, you drink from the well and think about your options. There aren't any, really. If the British find you, you'll become a prisoner because you fought for the Continentals. If the patriots find you, you'll be sold back into slavery. The only thing to do is go north. It is hundreds of miles to Canada. You start right away.

THE END

To follow another path, turn to page 9.
To read the conclusion, turn to page 99.

It feels wrong to attack a man you know, but you don't have much choice. You lift your ax and charge him. But suddenly he stops. He looks at you with recognition, hesitates, then ducks into a dark corridor. You follow him and find an open door. By the time you reach the door, he has already vanished into the trees. He escapes.

The battle in the outpost is over quickly. The British surrender, and you and the other sappers dig a new trench that brings the artillery ever closer to Yorktown. The cannons fire on the town, and after three days the British raise a white surrender flag. Eventually the guns stop firing and a British officer emerges. A drummer plays a parley. This is a signal that British General Cornwallis is ready is discuss the terms of surrender.

The two redcoats are brought back to camp. Cornwallis comes over to discuss with General Washington the terms of surrender. You witness all of this while standing guard. It is your first time seeing the patriot general in person. On the morning of October 19, the surrender is signed.

57

Acting for General Cornwallis, British Major General O'Hara presents his sword to General Washington in surrender.

Turn the page.

The next step is to evacuate all the British soldiers from the town. Hundreds of men march out and turn in their weapons. Among them, you see the man you recognized from the plantations. He sees you too, but he gives no gesture of recognition this time. He must be worried about his own fate. A slave who fought for the British and is captured by the patriots? There is no telling what Washington will do to him and the other slaves who made the same choice. He probably has a family back in Rhode Island, just as you do. What will happen to them? In another time and place, his family and yours could have been friends. Now you can only wonder what will happen.

THE END

To follow another path, turn to page 9.
To read the conclusion, turn to page 99.

It doesn't feel right to attack the man. Surely he joined the British for the same reason you joined the patriots. He thought it was his best chance at freedom. "Wait!" you say, lowering your weapon. When you do, he lunges at you with his bayonet, piercing it deep into your chest.

You realize the idea of sparing him was stupid. If an officer in your army saw you let him off, you would be severely punished. You would certainly not get your freedom. And the same goes for him. There are British soldiers and officers here. If they saw him spare an enemy, they would probably execute him.

You take out your mother's head cloth and press it to your bleeding chest. But it's too late. As you die you hope your mother finds freedom.

THE END

To follow another path, turn to page 9.
To read the conclusion, turn to page 99.

It's the food that tempts you the most. When rations run low, as they always do, the white soldiers eat first. You and the other black soldiers are constantly hungry. You unwrap a basket of biscuits and devour one. Then another. You tear off huge bites of salted meat and take long, delicious drinks of clean, fresh water. There is even milk! It all tastes so good.

At this point, you don't even care if you are thrown in prison until you die. This is the best day of your life. You take as many of the coins as you can hide in your uniform.

Later, in the streets, you see many dead civilians and soldiers. Many of them are black. You guess they were slaves who fled plantations to seek freedom with the British. But General Cornwallis forced the escaped slaves to fortify Yorktown.

Weakened and hungry, it appears that most of these people contracted smallpox and died before the siege even began. This food was here all along and could have helped them. One woman lies dead in a vegetable garden. Your breath catches in your throat for a second because she looks like your mother. But then you see that it is not her. It was just an illusion caused by the suffering of war.

After the war is over, you are freed as promised. You have a little money — your wages plus what you found in the courthouse. You plan to use it to help you return to Rhode Island. Thinking again of the woman in the garden, you hope that your mother is all right.

THE END

To follow another path, turn to page 9.
To read the conclusion, turn to page 99.

You don't want to risk stealing any of the spoils of war. If the white patriots caught you, who knows what they would do? So you report what you have found, even though you are extremely hungry.

With the fall of Yorktown, the British begin to lose their taste for war in America. It's not long before they withdraw. A treaty is negotiated in Paris, France, in which Great Britain agrees to American independence.

David Hartley, John Adams, Benjamin Franklin, and John Jay added their signatures and seals to the Treaty of Paris in 1783.

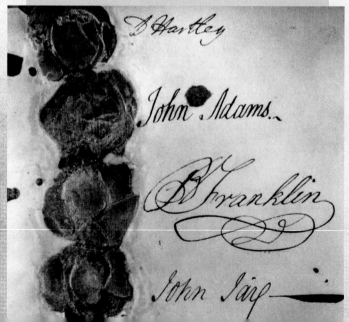

Suddenly, after so many years of fighting for the patriot cause, you are a free man. The nation is free of foreign rule too. You are paid wages for your duty and use them to return to Rhode Island. There you find that the old plantation has been ransacked and burned to the ground. You find a grave where your mother is buried. You don't know how she died. Whatever it was, you wish you could have been here. You feel awful for thinking about your own freedom while your mother needed you.

Alone, you go north to Boston and buy a ticket to sail to London. On your ship are a hundred or so other black men. They fought on both sides in the war. But you are not enemies here. You are brothers. Together you will seek a new life on the far side of the ocean.

THE END

To follow another path, turn to page 9.
To read the conclusion, turn to page 99.

You may never get a better chance than this. You stuff the food and money back inside the satchel and lift it off the dead man's body. Then you throw it across your shoulder and scamper into the woods.

Your shoulder hurts as you run. It's dark and a couple of times you trip over roots on the forest floor. By dawn you are far from camp, far from Yorktown, and far from danger. You decide to rest during the day, so you find a thick patch of leafy plants and curl up with the satchel for a pillow. You fall asleep to visions of life as a free man.

You wake up to a different vision. A white man on horseback looms above you. He is pointing a musket at you. "Get up," he says. You begin to stand and your injured arm shoots a shock of pain through your whole body.

Disregarding your pain, the man ties your hands behind your back, wrenching your bad shoulder. He takes the satchel and hides it inside his own, larger bag. He sits you on another horse and together you ride into a nearby town. You feel stupid for not having realized how close it was! The man takes you to an officer of some sort, who pays him. Then the man leaves. You sit in a jail cell and wait for what you are sure is coming: an auction. You will be sold back into slavery.

THE END

To follow another path, turn to page 9.
To read the conclusion, turn to page 99.

The war is going to end soon and you will be granted your legal freedom. It doesn't make sense to run now and live the rest of your life in fear of being captured. You make your way back to the camp, where your wound is dressed and your arm is set in a sling.

General Washington accepted the British surrender at Yorktown on October 19, 1781.

You have served for many years and sometimes you were not sure if you'd ever get out of the army. But finally it seems that your luck is turning. George Washington learns of your bravery during the Yorktown siege and personally presents you with a medal. You are told to rest for a few weeks. You can get back to fighting later. But by the time your arm heals, the war is over.

On your last day in service, you take your pay and your regular clothes and step into the street in New York. You are now standing in the United States of America — a free, independent man in a free, independent country.

It feels good.

THE END

To follow another path, turn to page 9.
To read the conclusion, turn to page 99.

CHAPTER 4

WAR HEROINE

You and your husband, Daniel Thomas, were married at the beginning of the revolution. Daniel is a cobbler with a small shop in New York City. You helped run the shop, learning the trade of repairing shoes and other leather goods.

At first you didn't pay much attention to the war. You focused on running your business. But as the revolution went on, your husband grew more patriotic. He felt it was his duty to help, so a year ago, he enlisted in the Continental Army. He left you to run the shop.

Turn the page.

At first things went well. But then the British took the city and redcoats began raiding the shop. They took shoes, leather, and money. They slept in your home. Finally you locked up and left the city. You found the camp where Daniel was, and you have been with the army ever since.

There are other women in camp who have done the same thing. General Washington does not like women being in camp — he says they distract the men and use up precious rations. You must walk instead of ride in the wagons. The army provides you with only half the rations that the men receive. But what Washington doesn't understand is what the women contribute to the army. You and the other women do laundry, sew clothing, cook meals, and nurse injuries. During battle, you have carried messages and supplies to troops. Daniel is in the artillery unit and you've even helped load and fire the cannons.

You do all this because you want to help your husband and the other men. But you have also come to support the patriotic cause. You are a fierce believer in American independence. But because of Washington's restrictions on food and wagon travel, you are weary and very hungry.

Now the army has arrived outside Yorktown. You help position the artillery and soon they begin firing on the town. The British return fire and the earth explodes where their shells land. While you are getting water for the men, a shell hits their trench. You return to find Daniel lying injured and unconscious. He is bleeding badly and his breath is shallow. Another man is clearly dead. A third man is the only one left on the cannon. He needs help.

To pull Daniel to safety and treat his injuries, turn to page 72.

To help with the cannon, turn to page 74.

You can't let your husband die. So you drag him through the trench. Explosions shake the ground and soldiers run frantically past. You move Daniel behind the lines to safety and lay him in the grass near a medical wagon. You tear off his shirt. His chest is covered in blood, so you get cloth from the wagon and a pitcher of water. His eyes spring open at the water's touch and he gasps. Then his eyes close again.

The wound is deep. Hoping to stop the bleeding, you begin to wrap his chest with the cloth. But before you finish, Daniel stops breathing. Your husband is dead.

With your hand pressed affectionately to his face, you allow yourself a moment of sadness. But a shell hits one of the wagons nearby and it explodes. You lean over Daniel's body to shield it from falling debris.

"Wounded coming!" someone yells. From the trenches you see several men carrying the injured toward you. You could be of great help to these men. At the same time, you are devastated with sadness. Your husband is gone and General Washington doesn't want you in camp. Maybe you should go home to the shop.

To go home, turn to page 77.

To stay and nurse the wounded, turn to page 91.

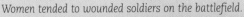

Women tended to wounded soldiers on the battlefield.

73

You feel sure Daniel will die no matter what you do. That is the sad but unavoidable fact. You know he would want you to keep fighting for the patriot cause.

So you load charge into the muzzle of the siege gun and stuff it down with the rammer. Next you load the shot — a solid cannonball meant to break apart the enemy's walls. Using the rammer, you stuff the shot all the way down. The other soldier, a man named Henry Ballinger, aims the gun and lights it. You both bend over and cover your ears, and seconds later it fires with a booming sound. The shot rips a hole in one of the wooden walls that the redcoats have erected for protection.

"Load another quickly!" says Ballinger.

Using the sponge — a long staff with cloth wrapped around the end — you scrub out the barrel. You must make sure no live gunpowder is still inside. Then you load another charge and another ball.

Kaboom!

It's another perfectly aimed shot and another big hole is torn open in the wall. There's no time to celebrate, though. A British shell explodes nearby, raining down debris. You dive under the cannon for protection.

You and Ballinger fire three more shots before Washington orders a stop. After the hours of earth-rattling explosions, the silence feels heavy and sad. Ballinger helps you carry your husband to join the other dead. He will be buried here at the battleground when the fighting is done.

Turn the page.

Meanwhile, General Washington himself approaches you. He gives his condolences for the loss of your husband. Then he surprises you with a compliment. "You fought bravely," he says. "I need someone with your courage and steady nerves to carry out a special mission. This person will deliver a secret letter to an undercover officer inside Yorktown." You feel thrilled to receive such a compliment, especially from a man who didn't want women in camp at all.

Ballinger and the other men would like you to keep fighting with the artillery unit. You have to agree that you and Ballinger make a great team.

To be Washington's spy, turn to page 80.
To stay with the artillery, turn to page 82.

Whatever patriotism you felt before has now dissolved. So you take Daniel's musket and food rations. You tell the pay officer to send his wages to New York. And you set off walking for home.

The rations last only a few days. You search for food in the forest, but the armies have stripped the trees bare. And then you pass a recent battleground. A redcoat lies dead under a tree. He has no food, but he does have money and ammunition. You take both. You scan the field for other supplies. It feels horrible, but you are desperate. You will die if you do not do it.

After another day of walking, you come to Williamsburg, Virginia. You have gathered enough money to buy a horse. You also eat a meal in a tavern and buy salted meat and biscuits for your journey. The rest of the trip home is much quicker and easier.

Turn the page.

But things aren't easy when you get there. Your home is still occupied by redcoats. You see them from the road and don't even approach the house. The shop has been ransacked. Even the shoe last, the stand on which a shoe is placed while you work on it, is gone. You have no choice but to return to your family's farm upstate.

Life is lonely and dull there — and you worry about the British. Will they come here looking for lodging and food? One day you do see a soldier come onto the land, but he's not British. He wears the tattered and bloody uniform of the Continental Army. It is clear that he has abandoned the army. They may be looking for him.

British soldiers occupied and took what they wanted from colonists' homes.

You point your musket at him as he approaches the house. "Get off my land," you say.

"Please," the man says. "I am starving and exhausted."

To take him in, turn to page 85.

To send him away, turn to page 87.

Later, at home in New York, you write a broadside — an argument that will be posted in public and passed around. In it you argue in favor of improved women's rights. "After all," you write, "we have fought for our country in the names of liberty and representation. Why not extend those ideas to all people? Women helped the war cause by taking on work set aside only for men. Some fought. Some worked in factories and fields and shops to supply the troops. Yet women are still considered inferior to men. They are not expected to be political or to earn equal wages. It is time to reconsider these old ideas."

84

In your lifetime you do not see improved pay or rights for women. But you do see the start of the discussion. For your role in that, you feel great pride.

THE END

To follow another path, turn to page 9.
To read the conclusion, turn to page 99.

You have seen the pain and suffering that war can cause. You cannot blame this man for running away. And he looks sick or injured — or both. He needs help and you can give it to him. And so you do.

You take the man inside and feed him a bowl of broth. His name is Gilbert. Your father does not like the idea of a soldier staying here, especially if he has deserted the army. Perhaps the authorities will be looking for him. "We must help him, father," you plead. "It is the kind thing to do."

Your father eventually agrees, but he was right about the authorities. Luckily, you see the soldiers coming and hide Gilbert in the forest behind the house. They search the farmhouse, but they don't find anything. After an hour, they leave.

Turn the page.

You bring Gilbert back inside and he thanks you again for your help. "I had better get out of here before they come back," he says. "I have a wife and family in Massachusetts. I want to get to them again."

That night, he sneaks out and goes back into the woods. You wish him good luck as he leaves.

The months go by. America wins the war. Life on the farm continues to be boring and predictable. You sell crops and save money and hope one day to reopen the cobbler shop. Then one day, you receive an anonymous package addressed from Massachusetts. A note inside says simply, "Thank you. I hope this will help you reopen your shop." The package contains money.

Gilbert, you think. *Thank you.*

THE END

To follow another path, turn to page 9.
To read the conclusion, turn to page 99.

You still believe in the patriotic cause and don't like the idea that someone would abandon the army. He does not deserve your help.

"I can't help you," you say. "Now go on — get out of here!"

Instead of leaving, though, he takes another step closer. You warn him again, but he comes even closer, so you shoot. He twists away, bleeding from the shoulder, and falls. He looks up at you with shock. His face is white. Blood stains the path. He gets unsteadily to his feet and runs away. He trips, falls, and gets up again, scampering into the woods.

You don't tell your father what happened, but you keep your musket ready in case the man returns. He doesn't come back and you begin to feel guilty for hurting him. You decide that you want to do something to help others.

Turn the page.

"Father," you say that night at dinner, "we must donate as much of our crop as possible to the Continental Army. The soldiers never have enough. We can help them."

Your father chews his potato for a moment, thinking, then replies. "We don't give anything away for free."

Before the war, you would have done what your father said. But now you feel stronger. More independent. "Well," you say, "this time we will."

He looks at you with shock, but he doesn't say anything else. And after the harvest, he helps you haul barrels of food into town where they will be delivered to the troops.

THE END

To follow another path, turn to page 9.
To read the conclusion, turn to page 99.

You don't want to take any chances, so you memorize the letter. Then you eat it. There is no way anyone will ever find it now!

Soon British guards on the outskirts of the town stop you. There are two of them, one with a dirty, curly beard. The red coats of their uniforms are dirty and torn. They look tired.

"What's your business in Yorktown?" one asks.

"To purchase a spade at the blacksmith," you reply.

The two men search your satchel and your pockets. They make you turn out your undergarments as well, but they find nothing.

"All right, then," says the one with the beard. Your heart is beating furiously as you walk away, trying to look calm. When you get around the corner and out of sight, you break into a run.

Turn the page.

You tell the blacksmith that you wish to purchase a spade. He looks around to make sure you're alone and he whispers, "Let's have it." You tell him that you memorized the letter and then you recite it. It concerns ship maneuvers in Chesapeake Bay. The blacksmith gives you a message to bring back to the general. He also gives you a spade. When you pass the guards on your way back out of town, they simply nod in recognition.

General Washington is pleased with your work and gives you another assignment. You complete that one as well. You find life as a spy to be a fulfilling way to serve the patriot cause. The only sad thing is that nobody knows your name. Your story will be lost to history.

THE END

To follow another path, turn to page 9.
To read the conclusion, turn to page 99.

You still want to help the patriot cause despite your grief and Washington's disrespect toward women. So you join the surgeon and nurses who are treating the injured. One man has a badly damaged forearm and you tie a tourniquet at his elbow. The surgeon saws off the lower arm and you bandage it up.

It goes like that for the rest of the battle. Some of the things you see are gruesome. They will haunt your dreams for the rest of your life. But the man whose arm was amputated lives and regains his health. This feels like a great victory.

After the battle, after the British surrender the town, you treat more sick and wounded soldiers. Some of them are British, but you help them anyway. You're beginning to think of yourself more as a nurse than a patriot. You help anyone in need.

Turn the page.

In the final weeks of the war and even as the peace treaty is being negotiated, you keep working. You still don't get enough food and the water you drink is often dirty. You are exposed to disease and filth and soon you develop a fever. The soldiers let you ride in a wagon despite Washington's order. They tell you how much they appreciate all you have done. You have treated many of them and some would not have lived without you. You are proud of the work you've done.

The fever does not go away and vomiting and diarrhea complicate it. You realize that you have dysentery. You may not live to see the birth of the new country.

THE END

To follow another path, turn to page 9.
To read the conclusion, turn to page 99.

92

You have to think fast. You decide to try to gain their affection.

"I'm an American, but I hate the patriots," you say. "This war has made me lose my shop. Fighting and disease are everywhere. I have no money, no family. Things were much better when Britain was in control. That's why I'm here. I want to volunteer to help. I can wash. I can mend clothes or cook."

This woman was arrested by the British while on her way to deliver a message from one patriot general to another.

The two men look at each other. They make a decision without speaking.

"All right," says the one with the beard. He waves a hand and you pass along.

You meet the blacksmith and deliver the message. He gives you a return message — and he gives you a spade.

That's right! You forgot that was your cover story. How can you get past the guards again with the spade when they think you are here to stay? You will have to find a different way out. You walk down a different street than the one you entered. Many people are lying in doorways, sick and dying. Most of them are black — former slaves who trusted the British with hopes of freedom. All they got was more hard work and now disease.

Finally, you find your way to a different entrance. Here, two other guards are stationed. On the horizon behind you, the sun is just beginning to rise. The artillery fire has died down for the moment. It seems almost peaceful.

"Where are you going?" one of the guards says roughly.

"To bury my husband," you say. "He was killed in the fighting."

"Drop the shovel," the other guard says. You do as you're told and they search you. They make you turn out your pockets and undergarments. Soon they find the blacksmith's letter and you are shackled and thrown in prison. Later that morning, you are hanged as a spy.

THE END

To follow another path, turn to page 9.
To read the conclusion, turn to page 99.

"I'm lost," you say. "I must find the blacksmith."

"Lost, eh?" says the bearded guard. He searches you and finds the letter. "What is this?" he asks.

As you watch him look at the letter, you can't believe your good luck. It appears the guard can't read. "It's a — it's a letter for my husband," you say.

The second guard has a rash all over his face and seems very ill. But he grabs the letter and looks at it. "I can read!" he says. As he scans the letter, his eyebrows rise. "Well, well," he says.

They take you to a small courthouse where you are locked in a cell. Before long, another man is brought into the cell too. He is a patriot officer — the blacksmith to whom the letter was addressed. You have not only gotten yourself captured, you are responsible for his capture too. You try to apologize, but he only scowls at you.

You are given no food or water. You realize it is only slightly worse treatment than you received when serving in the army camp. You grow weak and feverish. You are not sure what kind of illness you have.

Soon, the British surrender. Within a day the patriots come in to search. They find you and release you. The war is coming to an end. There is nothing left for you to do. You have no husband, shop, or money. You are sick. You have failed as a spy. You remember how happy you and Daniel were before the war began. The United States of America is an independent nation. But you wonder if you will ever find happiness in the new country.

THE END

To follow another path, turn to page 9.
To read the conclusion, turn to page 99.

CHAPTER 5

FROM SIEGE TO SURRENDER

In June 1781, George Washington and his army of about 3,000 were stationed outside New York City. The British had held it since 1776. Washington had the help of a 4,000-man French army led by General Rochambeau.

In July, the generals evaluated British defenses in New York. It seemed too well protected to attack. The British were entrenched with 14,000 troops. On August 14, word came that the French navy had sent 34 ships and 3,200 troops to the Chesapeake Bay. Washington decided that Yorktown, on the bay, would make a better target than New York.

Washington wanted the attack on Yorktown to be a surprise. So he left behind a small French army to build ovens in camp. Their goal was to make it look as though they were getting ready to attack New York. Washington also arranged for false attack plans to be intercepted by the British. He and Rochambeau started marching their armies south in late August. They took different routes to hide their numbers and allow for more opportunities to forage for food.

On August 29, the French ships arrived in Chesapeake Bay. On September 5, they engaged in a two-hour battle with the British. Both sides suffered casualties and neither lost a ship. But the French had more ships there and they sealed off the bay. The British ships retreated to New York. There would be no reinforcements for the British troops in Yorktown.

The allied armies met in Williamsburg in late September and marched together to Yorktown on September 28. Lord Cornwallis was the British general at Yorktown. He had a series of defensive outposts dug into the earth surrounding the town. On seeing the armies approaching, he abandoned the distant outposts and reinforced the ones closer to the town.

The allies dug zigzagging trenches to get closer to the town and fire their artillery. On October 9, the artillery bombardment began. The allies fired thousands of rounds into the town. Finally sappers were sent to cut through the abatis surrounding two of the outposts. Washington ordered the Continental Army and the French army to take the two outposts with bayonets and no shots fired. This would be an attack of stealth and speed. The outposts were quickly taken.

General Washington looks out over his men and the trenches dug outside of Yorktown.

This allowed trenches to be dug closer to the town. The British launched a counterattack against this trench, slowing the allied assault. But the attack was repelled and the assault continued. By this time, the end was in sight. The British fortifications in Yorktown were crumbling to pieces under the continuous artillery bombardment. On October 17 the British raised the white flag of surrender. An officer came out with a drummer beating a parley — a rhythm that told everyone they were coming to talk.

A surrender was signed on October 19. That afternoon the British marched out of the town and turned over their guns. The allies took 7,247 British soldiers and 840 sailors prisoner. They captured 244 cannons and other supplies.

After Yorktown, the British saw that they could not keep control of the American colonies. Peace negotiations began in April 1782.

Earlier in the war, the British had offered freedom to any slaves who joined them. Patriots tried to convince the slaves that they would be better off staying with their masters. It was a confusing and dangerous choice for enslaved people. They did not know if they would really be freed or what would happen if the patriots recaptured them. But many African-Americans took the offer and escaped to join the British.

General Washington resisted making a similar offer, partly because he and others feared the idea of armed African-Americans. But later, when the allies became desperate for more troops, some colonies began to recruit black soldiers. One of the most famous units to include black soldiers was the 1st Rhode Island regiment. The 1st Rhode Island fought bravely in several battles, including the Battle of Rhode Island. This regiment played a critical role at Yorktown.

During the war, women were often left at home while men went to battle. Some chose to follow the armies their husbands were in. Called "camp followers," they typically did the traditionally female jobs that kept the camps running: laundry, sewing, cooking, and nursing. Sometimes they were paid a little money and other times they were paid nothing.

Food was always in short supply and often the women in camps would get little or no food. The idea was that the soldiers needed the food more. Women often had no choice but to scavenge battlefields and take anything of value they could find from fallen soldiers.

General Washington regarded women in camp as a burden and would not allow them to ride in the wagons. He did not see the value they provided. After the war, many women petitioned the army for back wages and recognition for the work they did. Working with the armies and alone at shops and on farms led many women to feel newly independent and capable. Some began to challenge the traditional roles that were expected of women. These were some of the challenges that faced the newly independent United States.

TIMELINE

August 14, 1781—American General George Washington learns that French ships are sailing to the Chesapeake Bay

August 19—Washington begins to secretly move the allied armies south

September 5—The French ships defeat the British ships at Chesapeake Bay, sealing off the navy and preventing British reinforcements from arriving at Yorktown

September 14—Washington and French General Rochambeau arrive in Williamsburg, Virginia

September 28—Patriot and French armies march out of Williamsburg to Yorktown

October 6—Sappers begin digging zigzagging trenches to approach Yorktown

October 9—The allies begin shelling Yorktown

October 14—Patriot and French infantry seize two British outposts; the allies begin digging a new trench

October 16, daytime—The British launch a failed counterattack against artillery in the new trench

October 16, evening—British General Cornwallis attempts to escape with his army by boat, but a storm sets them back

October 17—The British raise the white flag, signaling their intent to surrender

October 19—Surrender terms are signed, effectively ending the war

OTHER PATHS TO EXPLORE

In this book, you've seen how events from the past look different from three points of view. Perspectives on history are as varied as the people who lived it. Seeing history from many points of view is an important part of understanding it. Here are ideas for other Revolutionary War points of view to explore:

+ What are some of the ways that women began to push for greater rights and recognition following the Revolutionary War? Support your answer with examples from at least two other texts or valid Internet sources.

+ The American Revolution forced American colonists to decide between supporting the patriots or the British. Historians estimate that about 20 percent of colonists were loyalists — people who remained loyal to England. How might a person's individual experiences have influenced his or her decision to support one side or the other during the war?

READ MORE

Bradford, James C. *The American Revolution: A Visual History.* New York: DK Publishing, 2016.

Raum, Elizabeth. *At Battle in the Revolutionary War: An Interactive Battlefield Adventure.* North Mankato, Minn.: Capstone Press, 2015.

Raum, Elizabeth. *Spies of the American Revolution: An Interactive Espionage Adventure.* North Mankato, Minn.: Capstone Press, 2016.

INTERNET SITES

Use FactHound to find Internet sites related to this book.

Visit *www.facthound.com*

Just type in 9781543502893 and go.

GLOSSARY

abatis (AB-uh-tee)—a defensive object formed by a cut-off treetop with branches sharpened into spikes

amputation (am-pyuh-TAY-shun)—the removal of an arm, leg, or other body part, usually because the part is damaged

artillery (ar-TIL-uh-ree)—cannons and other large guns used during battles

bayonet (BAY-uh-net)—a long metal blade attached to the end of a musket or rifle and used in hand-to-hand combat

infantry (IN-fuhn-tree)—a group of people in the military trained to fight on land

plantation (plan-TAY-shuhn)—a large farm where crops such as cotton and sugarcane are grown; before 1865, plantations were run by slave labor

redcoat (RED-coht)—British soldiers, named after the color of their uniforms

sapper (SA-puhr)—someone in the military who specializes in field work

smallpox (SMAWL-poks)—a deadly disease that spreads easily from person to person, causing chills, fever, and pimples that scar

BIBLIOGRAPHY

Davis, Kenneth C. *The Hidden History of America at War: Untold Tales from Yorktown to Fallujah.* New York: Hachette Books, 2015.

Ketchum, Richard M. *Victory at Yorktown: The Campaign That Won the Revolution.* New York: Henry Holt, 2004.

Middlekauff, Robert. *The Glorious Cause: The American Revolution, 1763–1789.* New York: Oxford University Press, 2005.

Raphael, Ray. *A People's History of the American Revolution: How Common People Shaped the Fight for Independence.* New York: Perennial, 2002.

Wood, Gordon S. *The American Revolution: A History.* New York: Modern Library, 2002.

INDEX

abatis, 15, 19, 20, 22, 23, 24, 26, 32, 34, 44, 45, 50, 101

African American soldiers, 41, 42, 49, 54–55, 58, 60, 63, 64–65, 94, 103–104

amputations, 91

artillery, 15–16, 28, 32, 36, 38, 39, 43, 44, 45, 46, 51, 52, 53, 54, 56, 70, 71, 74–75, 76, 82, 95, 101, 102, 107

Battle of Rhode Island, 44, 104

bayonets, 19, 22, 33, 35, 36, 43, 46, 47, 49, 59, 101

British army, 8, 34, 37, 38, 44, 47, 48, 49, 50, 51, 56, 58, 59, 70, 83, 91, 97, 99, 102–103, 107

British navy, 8, 12, 14, 28, 100, 106

broadsides, 84

Continental army, 14, 15, 18, 30, 41, 55, 69, 70, 78, 88, 99, 101, 106, 107

Cornwallis, Lord, 28, 37, 51, 57, 60, 101, 107

desertion, 23, 24, 34, 53, 54–55, 64–65, 78–79, 85–86, 87

dysentery, 92

1st Rhode Island regiment, 47, 104

food, 14, 16, 21, 48, 51, 60, 61, 64, 70, 71, 77, 78, 88, 92, 97, 100, 105

French army, 11–12, 14, 15, 30, 99, 100, 101, 106, 107

French navy, 8, 12, 99, 100, 106

Hamilton, Alexander, 19, 32, 36

New York City, 12, 17, 67, 69, 70, 99, 100

nurses, 91

outposts, 15, 19, 21–24, 32, 33, 34, 35, 36, 38, 44, 45, 46, 47, 49, 50, 54, 56, 82, 101, 107

parley, 56, 102

plantations, 48, 49, 52, 55, 58, 60, 63

prisoners, 15–16, 27, 28, 36, 47, 54, 55, 103

raids, 48, 70, 78

Rochambeau, General, 12, 26, 27, 28, 33, 99, 100, 106

sappers, 19, 20, 22, 23, 24, 32, 36, 38, 43, 44, 45, 46, 50, 54, 56, 82, 101, 106

smallpox, 16, 29, 30, 31, 61

spies, 17, 29, 76, 80, 81, 82, 89–90, 93–95, 96–97

surgeons, 91

surrender, 28, 34, 37, 47, 51, 56–57, 83, 91, 97, 102, 103, 107

Treaty of Paris, 62

trenches, 17, 36, 38, 43, 50, 51, 52, 53, 54, 56, 71, 73, 82, 101, 102, 106, 107

Washington, George, 7, 8, 12, 15, 19, 21, 22, 32, 33, 36, 37, 39, 44, 46, 51, 57, 58, 67, 70, 71, 73, 75, 76, 80, 82, 83, 90, 91, 92, 99–100, 101, 104, 105, 106

women, 70, 76, 82, 83, 84, 91, 104–105